BUSES OF SHROPSHIRE AND MID WALES

JOHN LAW

AMBERLEY

First published 2021

Amberley Publishing
The Hill, Stroud
Gloucestershire, GL5 4EP

www.amberley-books.com

Copyright © John Law, 2021

The right of John Law to be identified as
the Author of this work has been asserted in
accordance with the Copyrights, Designs and
Patents Act 1988.

ISBN 978 1 4456 9569 3 (print)
ISBN 978 1 4456 9570 9 (ebook)

British Library Cataloguing in Publication Data.
A catalogue record for this book is available from
the British Library.

Origination by Amberley Publishing.
Printed in the UK.

Introduction

Shropshire is a mainly rural area of England, with its county town being Shrewsbury. Other important towns include Bridgnorth, Ludlow and Oswestry. The new town of Telford has been growing in prominence as it engulfs Wellington and its environs. That area was fundamental to the early days of the Industrial Revolution.

The people of Mid Wales have long used Shrewsbury and Shropshire as their main access point into England. Likewise, residents of the West Midlands and beyond have travelled in the opposite direction to reach the coast at Aberystwyth and its nearby resorts. For the purposes of this book, Mid Wales includes Welshpool, Newtown, Machynlleth and Aberystwyth, a natural corridor separating North and South Wales.

Much of Shropshire in the 1970s was the domain of Midland Red, the huge Birmingham-based National Bus Company subsidiary. It was split up in the early 1980s in preparation for privatisation, with Midland Red North becoming the county's major operator.

The Oswestry area, plus all of Mid Wales, was similarly dominated by Crosville Motor Services, a former Tilling Group business. The fleet consisted mainly of Bristol/ECW types, at least until the introduction of the Leyland National. Again, anticipating future events, the company was split, with Crosville Wales taking over. Both Midland Red North and Crosville Wales were sold and eventually became part of Arriva – the situation today.

At this point it should be mentioned that Crosville Wales' only English operations, based in Oswestry, later passed to Midland Red North. Also Midland Red West's buses could be found in parts of Shropshire, as it had a depot in Bridgnorth. Potteries Motor Traction's buses could also be seen in Shrewsbury, running from Hanley via Market Drayton. First Bus is the successor to these operations.

However, most bus enthusiasts did not flock to Shropshire and Mid Wales to see the vehicles of Crosville or Midland Red. These mainly standardised buses could be much more easily be found in places like Chester or Birmingham. It was probably the independent companies that provided the most interest.

One of the most fondly remembered was Vaggs Coaches, based at the delightfully named village of Knockin Heath. A fine collection of vehicles was used on the stage services, while a visit to the depot would usually reveal a few withdrawn gems gradually rotting away in the yard. Sadly, Vaggs ceased trading in the early 1980s.

Salopia Saloon Coaches of Whitchurch started out in 1915 and grew to become a significant player in the Shropshire bus scene. The company sold out to Shearings in 1979 with that firm's buses becoming a regular sight in the county until stage carriage services were disposed of.

Shropshire also provided Minsterley Motors, still trading today, having taken over the routes of Valley Motor Services, serving the fine town of Bishop's Castle.

Around Wellington and the rapidly growing Telford new town, a host of small independents had bonded together to form the Shropshire Omnibus Association. This lasted until 1978, when Midland Red took over most of the operations.

Another notable independent was Hampson's, who ran the Oswestry town service. Ex-London Transport RF type AEC Regal IV saloons were in use in the 1970s. In addition, the area was served by Parish of Morda plus Owen's Coaches, from just over the border.

Mid Wales Motorways, once based at the largest town in Powys, Newtown, once served much of the border area. In 1988 it was taken over by Evans Coaches of Aberystwyth, who still use the name for operations in the area.

Perhaps the biggest of the Welsh independent operators today is Lloyds Coaches of Machynlleth, having taken over the former Arriva depot and services in the town. The company also participates in the TrawsCymru network covering much of rural Wales.

Many of the area's smaller operators have fallen by the wayside, including Cross Gates Coaches of Mid Wales, Whittle's of Highley and Williamson's from Shrewsbury. Others, such as Tanat Valley, have been in business for 100 years and are still going strong.

Put together, the area of Shropshire and Mid Wales has long been an area of great interest to bus enthusiasts and long may it continue to do so.

The author is grateful to the following for supplying a few photographs: Barrie Gilbert, Steve Guess, the late Keith Holt, Richard Huggins, Jim Sambrooks and Malcolm Yeomans. Thanks are also due to 'Bus Lists on the Web' for providing much of the information, saving the author hours of trawling through various fleet lists.

Midland Red was the dominant bus operator in Shrewsbury and Northern Shropshire for many years. The company once manufactured its own vehicles, including the famous D9 double-decker. On 29 May 1973, No. 5027 (3027 HA), a fine example of the type, was photographed at rest in Hills Lane, Shrewsbury. Its Midland Red-built bodywork featured, as standard, platform doors and room for seventy-two seated passengers. The pre-National Bus Company (NBC) livery is still applied. (Malcolm Yeomans)

Midland Red also built its own single-deck vehicles. Here, in the foreground, is S17 type fifty-two-seat saloon No. 5450 (6450 HA) at Shrewsbury on 3 March 1974. Behind is Leyland Leopard/ Willowbrook No. 5215 (5215 HA). Both buses were delivered in 1963. (The late Keith Holt)

Midland Red later purchased 'off the peg' standard buses, including large amounts of Daimler Fleetlines, one of which is seen in Bridgnorth in September 1976. Now wearing NBC 'poppy red' paintwork, 6123 (LHA 623F) carries Alexander seventy-seven-seat bodywork. (Steve Guess)

In 1981, Midland Red was split up, with most of the Shropshire operations becoming Midland Red North. Though still under NBC control, this was in preparation for privatisation and deregulation. One of the first new vehicles for Midland Red North was found at Shrewsbury depot in spring 1984. No. 1702 (A702 HVT) was one of a batch of nine Duple Dominant-bodied Leyland Tiger buses, seating fifty-one passengers. It is seen carrying 'Hotspur' branding for local services. After withdrawal in 1999, this vehicle passed to Aberystwyth operator Mid Wales Travel.

Also photographed with 'Hotspur' names is Midland Red North 812 (BVP 812V), a Leyland National 2 forty-nine-seat saloon that had been new to Midland Red in 1980. It is seen at the old bus station in Shrewsbury in mid-1985.

Wearing 'Tellus' branding for Telford area operations, Midland Red North Mark I Leyland National No. 766 (BVP 766V) is seen in Bridgnorth High Street on 19 March 1988, with the town's sole surviving gateway behind. Bought by Midland Red in 1979, along with many others, this forty-nine-seat bus is loading up for a trip to Wolverhampton. (Richard Huggins)

Another typical ex-Midland Red vehicle, No. 359 (GOH 359N) is a Leyland Leopard with dual-purpose Marshall bodywork. Despite its 'Tellus' identification, it is about to depart from Shrewsbury on an X64 duty to Hanley via Market Drayton.

With both 'Hotspur' and 'ME' (Midland Express) branding, Midland Red North 1502 (ANA 91Y) was photographed in Shrewsbury's old bus station in mid-1985. This ECW coach-bodied Leyland Leopard had been new to National Travel (West) and would have been ideal for the journey it was about to operate: the X96 to Birmingham.

With privatisation looming, most NBC subsidiaries began to develop their own identities and liveries. Wearing its new colours in late 1987 is Midland Red North 1436 (WOC 736T), a 1979-built Leyland Leopard/Plaxton coach. It had originally been No. 736 in the Midland Red fleet. It was photographed outside the depot in Wellington in late 1987.

Painted all white, with 'Hotspur' names, Midland Red North No. 1507 (SOH 554Y) had been recently transferred from Midland Red (Express) when photographed in Shrewsbury in mid-1987. This Plaxton Paramount-bodied Leyland Tiger had been new in 1983.

Like most of Britain's bus companies, Midland Red North began to purchase minibuses in the mid-1980s. One of the first examples was No. 18 (C318 URF), a Ford Transit/Dormobile sixteen-seater. It is seen in Shrewsbury bus station in mid-1987.

A slightly later version of the Ford Transit minibus with Midland Red North is seen here, at the small bus station in Oakengates in late 1987. No. 95 (D95 CFA) is another sixteen-seat Dormobile-finished vehicle. Midland Red North was sold to the Drawlane Group in January 1988.

The date is now 15 June 1989 and Midland Red North has new owners. Two minibuses are seen in Shrewsbury bus station sporting their new colours. The vehicle on the left is 234 (E234 NFX), a Freight Rover Sherpa/Carlyle twenty-seat minibus that had previously been owned by Shamrock & Rambler (Charlie's Cars) of Dorset. To its right is 308 (F608 EHA), a new Iveco 49.10/Carlyle B23F vehicle. (Richard Huggins)

Looking smart in its recently acquired livery is Midland Red North 469 (JOX 469P). This coach had entered the Midland Red fleet as a new Leyland Leopard with Plaxton Supreme Express coachwork in 1976. It was photographed on a sunny summer's day in Shrewsbury, 1989.

Midland Red North 575 (NOE 575R), a former Midland Red forty-three-seat Leyland National, is seen in central Shrewsbury on 15 June 1989. Operating a local service, it bears the fleet name of 'Hotspur Midland Red'. The company used 'Midland Red' or 'Midland' names until it became part of Arriva. (Richard Huggins)

The 1990s saw Midland Red North receive larger minibuses, more suitable for the needs of its passengers. At Shrewsbury's new bus station in the spring of 1991 we see No. 332 (H332 DHA), a Northern Counties-bodied Renault Dodge S56 with twenty-three seats.

By late 1992, the Crosville Wales depot in Oswestry had passed to Midland Red North, with the name 'Cambrian Midland Red' being employed. Carrying that lettering is C253 SPC, a London Country South West Duple 320-bodied Leyland Tiger that was on loan from the fellow Drawlane/British Bus Group company. It was photographed at the Oswestry premises in December 1992.

By the time of this photograph, spring 1995, Midland Red North had adopted this dark red livery, seen applied to No. 448 (F148 USX). At first glance, this is just one of many larger minibuses in the fleet, but it had been new to Scottish operator Mitchell's of Plean. It is an Alexander-bodied Mercedes 811D and was photographed passing the Albert pub in Shrewsbury – very handy for the new bus station.

For Shrewsbury park & ride duties a special yellow and blue colour scheme was in use, shown
to good effect on 804 (M804 MOJ). Delivered in late 1994, it is a Marshall-bodied forty-seat
Dennis Dart and is seen turning in to Shrewsbury's new bus station in spring 1995.

Another view of a Midland Red North vehicle about to enter Shrewsbury bus station in spring
1995. This time the vehicle is No. 937 (PUK 637R), an East Lancs 'Greenway' conversion of
former Midland Red Leyland National 637.

Again, it is spring 1995 and Midland Red North No. 1404 (M404 EFD) is in Shrewsbury park & ride colours operating the Meole Brace route as it passes along Smithfield Road on the edge of the town centre. Purchased in April 1994, it is a Scania N113CRL with East Lancs forty-two-seat bodywork.

With Shrewsbury's new bus station visible on the right, Midland Red North 1209 (G309 DPA) is seen having just departed in spring 1995. This Dennis Falcon with East Lancs bodywork had originally been delivered to London Country South West. Vaggs Coaches and other operators once used the parking area in the left background as a terminal point.

In the later years of Midland Red North, the company re-employed the yellow and red colour scheme. Former park & ride bus 804 (M804 MOJ) – see page 14 – is painted in that livery as it departs Shrewsbury bus station in spring 1998. By then the company had started to rebrand itself as Arriva and we will look at that concern's vehicles after seeing those of the region's other major operator, Crosville Motor Services.

Crosville Motor Services employed a fleet that, in the 1970s and 1980s, consisted of mainly Bristol/ECW types. The company did, however, have some Leyland Leopard coaches, with Plaxton Elite Express bodywork. One of them, No. ELL317 (RMA 317P), was photographed at Aberystwyth depot in 1981. Note the 'De Cambria' branding, a result of the 'Market Analysis Project' that brought about local area identities.

Also with 'De Cambria' lettering, No. ERG160 (EFM 160H), a 1970-built Bristol RELH6G with forty-seven-seat ECW coachwork, is looking smart in dual-purpose livery at Aberystwyth depot in 1981.

In the 1970s, Sheffield Transport bought a small batch of Bristol VRT/SL6G double-deckers with East Lancs bodywork. They did not find favour in Yorkshire, so six were purchased by Crosville. One of them, numbered HVG932 (OWE 272K), was found at Aberystwyth depot in 1981.

Very much a standard double-deck vehicle with Crosville, DVG517 (YMB 517W) was one of
many Bristol VRT/SL3/6LXB types in the fleet, bodied by ECW, of course. Delivered in June
1981, it is seen in Aberystwyth shortly afterwards, with lettering celebrating seventy-five years
of the company.

Outside Crosville's Oswestry depot in 1982 we see Bristol VRT/SL6G double-decker DVG542
(SCD 504H). It is fitted with the earlier style of ECW bodywork and had been new to Southdown
Motor Services in 1970.

By the summer of 1987, when this photograph was taken, Crosville Motor Services had been split into two. Crosville Cymru/Crosville Wales had been formed to take over the Welsh operations, plus Oswestry depot in Shropshire, England. It is here that we see SRG208 (HFM 208J), a 1970-built Bristol RELL6G/ECW saloon, still in NBC green, with its new fleet names.

Now wearing its new Crosville Cymru colours, No. ENL926 (HFM 182N) is seen at Shrewsbury in the summer of 1987. This 1975-built Leyland National was fitted with forty-eight dual-purpose seats.

Photographed at Oswestry in summer 1987 was Crosville Cymru DVL411 (ODM 411V), a standard Bristol VRT/SL3/501 with seventy-four-seat ECW bodywork.

Crosville Cymru DOG194 (B194 BLG) is seen having just departed from its Shrewsbury stand for Oswestry in summer 1987. This Leyland Olympian/ECW bus had been new, with the same fleet number, to Crosville in 1985. The three letters 'DOG' stood for 'Double-deck', 'Olympian' and 'Gardner' (the engine manufacturer).

Like most other operators, Crosville Cymru turned to the minibus for its fleet requirements in the late 1980s/early 1990s. At Aberystwyth in March 1995 we see two of them, both Ivecos. On the left is MCF281 (F81 CJC), a 49.10S bodied by Carlyle; while to its right we have MIF290 (M290 AJC), a later 59.12/Marshall twenty-seven-seat vehicle.

In 1997 both Crosville Cymru and Midland Red North were rebranded as Arriva, with a common blue livery being introduced. Proudly displaying its new colours is No. 799 (J328 VAW), a Carlyle-bodied Dennis Dart that had been acquired from Williamson's, a local independent, in 1998. It is seen in Shrewsbury bus station in the summer of 1999, when a repainting programme was at its halfway stage.

No. 1341 (R341 TJW) in the Arriva fleet had come from Midland Red North, having been delivered in early 1998. This Dennis Dart SLF had Plaxton bodywork seating thirty-nine passengers and was photographed in Shrewsbury bus station in July 1999.

Here is a view of the former Crosville Cymru depot in Machynlleth in Arriva's hands in March 2001. On the left can be seen MMM862 (the Crosville fleet numbering system was still in use then), registered R962 FYS. This Mellor-bodied Mercedes 810D had been new to a North Wales operator from the Bethesda area. To its right is SLG312 (G312 DPA), an ex-London & Country Leyland Lynx.

Inside Machynlleth depot in March 2001 is Arriva CTC69 (IIL 9169). This Plaxton-bodied Leyland Tiger coach had been new to the Shearings organisation in 1988 registered F710 ENE. It was sold to GHA Coaches in 2003. Machynlleth depot was later closed and taken over by Lloyds Coaches.

Arriva's No. 1026 (F281 AWW), a Leyland Lynx, is seen leaving Shrewsbury bus station in March 2001. This had been new to Yorkshire Woollen District as No. 281 in 1988.

The author's visit to Shropshire in March 2001 coincided with a spell of inclement weather. A visit to Telford's new bus station saw some cold conditions as Arriva No. 501 (H501 GHA), a thirty-five-seat Dennis Dart/East Lancs saloon, awaits departure time.

A more unusual Dennis Dart in the Arriva fleet in Shropshire was No. 524 (J556 GTP), with a Wadham Stringer body, seating thirty-five passengers. It had originally been a demonstrator for the bodybuilder. Here, it is seen leaving Shrewsbury bus station in March 2001.

The summer of 1999 provided much better conditions for photography as Arriva 917 (JOX 517P) was captured on film at Shrewsbury. This Leyland National had been new to Midland Red in 1976.

Another Leyland National, this time a Mark 2 type, Arriva No. 825 (DOC 26V) is seen in Shrewsbury in March 2001. This bus had started life as No. 1026 in the West Midland PTE fleet. Today it is preserved, fully restored to its original colours, at the Transport Museum at Wythall.

Here is another Dennis Dart in the Arriva fleet, this time a step-entrance SFD4 type with Plaxton bodywork, No. 1328 (P828RWU), photographed in Aberystwyth on 25 July 2007. It had been transferred from Arriva's South London fleet.

Back to Telford bus station in March 2001 and another second-hand bus in the Arriva fleet. No. 539 (G217 LGK), a Duple-bodied Dennis Dart, had been new to London operator R&I Tours.

Arriva's Shropshire fleet seemed to like collecting pre-owned Dennis Darts. Here is another one, No. 551 (H851 NOC) with Carlyle bodywork. It had come from Thanet Bus of Ramsgate, where it had provided competition for Stagecoach's East Kent operations. Shrewsbury bus station, March 2001.

Arriva Cymru's fleet No. SSC303 (F303 MNK) was photographed in Aberystwyth in March 2001. This unusual Wadham Stringer-bodied Leyland Swift had been transferred from the former Luton & District operation.

Another transferred-in vehicle to Arriva's Welsh operation, DOL103 (A103 OUG), was also found in Aberystwyth in March 2001. This Northern Counties-bodied Leyland Olympian had been new to South Yorkshire Road Transport of Pontefract as fleet No. 103. It is nice to report that it has since been preserved in Scotland and given the nickname 'Rosie'.

By March 2001 the low-floor era had reached Arriva's Shropshire area. In Oakengates bus station is No. 2233 (V233 KDA), a 2000-built Volvo B6BLE with Wright thirty-six-seat bodywork.

The TrawsCymru services form a network of connecting routes covering most of Wales, particularly links between north and south, as there are no parallel railways. Various operators are involved and, on 25 July 2007, Arriva's 2863 (YJ55 BKN) was photographed leaving Aberystwyth for Aberteifi (Cardigan in English). This dual-purpose Optare Tempo forty-one-seat saloon had been new in 2005.

Arriva No. 2359 (N238 VPH) is seen about to enter Shrewsbury bus station on a local duty on 6 October 2010. Thirty-one-seat East Lancs bodywork features on a Dennis Dart SLF chassis. It had been new to London & Country in 1996.

The Optare Versa has found favour with Arriva's Shropshire operations. An example, thirty-eight-seat No. 2990 (YJ09 MKD), was photographed on 6 October 2010, having just left Shrewsbury bus station.

Some vehicles in Arriva's fleet are painted in Shropshire County Council's blue livery for dedicated duties. Wearing park & ride branding is 2303 (N303 ENX), a Dennis Dart SLF with Plaxton bodywork featuring dual-purpose seating. Shrewsbury, 7 October 2010.

Twenty-six-seat Optare Solo No. 6000 (BU03 HRL) was also photographed in Shropshire CC blue, as it was about to enter Shrewsbury bus station on 5 October 2010.

Midland Red West also operated into Shropshire, with services mainly originating in neighbouring Worcestershire. At Shrewsbury in the summer of 1987 we see 451 (JOX 451P). In its latest colours, it is a Leyland Leopard/Plaxton forty-nine-seat coach, about halfway on its journey on the X55 Cardiff to Liverpool service.

Midland Red West was later absorbed into First Group and wearing that livery in Ludlow on 4 October 2010 is 42402 (P402 MLA). This Plaxton-bodied Dennis Dart SLF had originated with Centrewest in London.

Potteries Motor Traction (PMT), later to become part of First Bus, regularly served Shrewsbury by means of the hourly X64 service from Hanley, via Market Drayton. Having a rest at its westerly terminus in March 2001 is Leyland Lynx saloon No. 854 (H854 GRE), still in PMT colours but clearly under First ownership. Today the X64 is operated by Arriva.

First Cymru could also be seen in Mid Wales, having a share of the TrawsCymru express services. Branded as now obsolete 'Traws Cambria', Optare Tempo saloon 64503 (YJ55 BJK) is seen on arrival in Aberystwyth on 25 July 2007. This vehicle later passed to Richard Brothers of Pembrokeshire for continued use on such duties.

The Stagecoach Group also had services as part of the Traws Cambria network. Again, Optare Tempo vehicles were employed, including thirty-eight-seat example No. 25102 (YJ55 YFZ). On 11 October 2006 it was photographed in Llandrindod Wells on a Brecon to Newtown working.

Another major operator – albeit a short-lived one – to serve Mid Wales was French-owned Veolia. In that company's red colour scheme is twenty-nine-seat Optare Solo CN07 KZJ. Seen in Aberystwyth on 25 July 2007, this vehicle had been new to Bebb of Llantwit Fardre in South Wales.

Salopia Saloon Coaches started trading in 1915, from a base in Whitchurch, Shropshire. Regular services into Shrewsbury were soon part of the company's portfolio and, in the mid-1970s, SNT 284H was a regular performer on such duties. This Willowbrook-bodied Bedford VAM70 is seen in the old Shrewsbury bus station.

Here is another of Salopia's Bedford/Willowbrook combinations: UNT 291J, a YRQ with forty-five dual-purpose seats, new to the company in 1971. Again, it was photographed at Shrewsbury bus station circa 1975.

In 1979 Salopia sold out to Shearings, a large coach firm based in north-west England, who continued to run the various bus services in and around Shropshire. In 1987, in Whitchurch, we see ex-Burnley & Pendle Leyland National No. 43 (YCW 843N).

Another second-hand vehicle in the Shearings fleet is seen arriving at Telford new town's bus station in the summer of 1990. No. 126 (G350 GCK), a Duple-bodied Dennis Dart, had originally been a demonstrator and the paintwork still shows evidence of that employment. Shearings has recently ceased trading, though bus service provision had already long been given up.

The Shropshire Omnibus Association (SOA) was formed by an assortment of operators pooling their vehicles to provide bus services around the Wellington and Telford area. Each company used their own liveried buses, as we can see on this example in the Martlew's fleet, registered UUJ 394. This Duple Midland-bodied Bedford SB1, built in 1960, had been new to another SOA operator, Smith's Eagle. It was photographed at its Donnington terminus in 1975.

Brown's of Donnington Wood was another SOA business, once famous for its Sentinel vehicles. By the mid-1970s a more conventional Bedford YRQ/Willowbrook forty-five-seat bus, VUJ 252J, was in use. It was photographed at the depot. (From an original transparency in author's collection)

Until the full development of Telford new town, most of the local bus services centred on Wellington, where one street served as a terminus. Picking up passengers outside the Midland Red office in 1975 is Ashley's (another SOA partner) HFA 208E. New to Victoria Motorways of the Burton-upon-Trent area, it is a Strachans-bodied Bedford VAM5.

Ashley's DUX 773L had been new to another Shropshire operator, Vaggs Coaches, in 1973. By 1975 however, this Duple Dominant-bodied Ford R1014 was photographed on stage carriage work in Wellington.

R. A. Price, another SOA participant, was using CWU 185H on service when photographed in Wellington in 1975. This Ford R192 with Plaxton Derwent forty-five-seat dual-purpose bodywork had been new in 1970 to Doncaster area bus company Premier of Stainforth.

One of the best known of the SOA companies was Smith's Eagle of Trench. Photographed in Wellington in 1975 and operating one of the services to Donnington was VTG 739, a Bedford SB8 with Duple Midland bodywork. It had originally been delivered to South Wales business Thomas of Barry.

Resplendent in the green and cream livery of Smith's Eagle, KUP 889J is seen in the sun in the mid-1970s at its Donnington terminus. A Bedford VAM70/Willowbrook bus, it had come from County Durham operator Martindale of Ferryhill. (From an original transparency in author's collection)

Pressed into SOA stage carriage duties in the mid-1970s is Smith's Eagle-owned WUJ 902. An AEC Reliance with forty-one-seat Duple Britannia coachwork, it was photographed at Donnington. (From an original transparency in author's collection)

Another Smith's Eagle coach, AAW 411K, was photographed in the mid-1970s in a Telford housing estate, on stage carriage work (and *not* bound for Blackpool). The vehicle is a Plaxton-bodied Leyland Leopard bought new in 1972. Most of the Shropshire Omnibus Association services were sold to Midland Red in 1978.

The Whittle firm can trace its roots back to 1926. For many years the company ran a Bridgnorth to Kidderminster service via Highley, where the depot was situated. Seen in Highley sometime around 1975 is PUX 705M, a Bedford YRT with fifty-three-seat Duple Dominant bodywork, fitted with folding doors for stage carriage work.

In July 1995, Whittle's K6 GOW was photographed in central Bridgnorth. This Northern Counties-bodied Dennis Dart had been new to the company in 1992. It has just come under the town's Northgate gateway and will take up a service to Kidderminster.

With the beginning of tendering for non-profitable bus routes, Whittle gained a few services beyond its normal sphere of operations. Seen in Shrewsbury in March 2001 is V930 EWP, a Dennis Dart SPD/Plaxton forty-one-seat bus. It had been new in 1999.

Also photographed in March 2001, Optare Solo twenty-nine-seat saloon X147 JWP is operating a local route in Ludlow. In 2004, the Whittle Company was sold to East Yorkshire Motors Services, but was passed on to Johnson's of Henley-in-Arden. Bus service work is no longer undertaken.

One of the author's favourite operators was Hampson's Luxury Coaches of Oswestry. As well as some rural services, the company also operated a town service, which was the normal duty for a pair of ex-London Transport 'Private Hire' type AEC Regal IV 'RF' types. One of them, No. 21 (LUC 213), a 1951-built bus with Metro-Cammell bodywork, is seen in the town centre in 1975.

No. 27 in the Hampson's fleet, registered TUJ 421J, is seen near to Oswestry town centre sometime around 1974. New to the company in 1970, it is a Bedford SB5 with a Willowbrook body containing thirty-nine dual-purpose seats.

One of the 'Luxury Coaches' in the Hampson fleet, 28 (UUX 356), was photographed at the depot circa 1975. This fine Bedford SB1 with Duple 'Super Vega' coachwork had been with the company since being delivered in 1960.

In its later years, Hampson's appeared to have ceased using fleet numbers. BNU 676G is the subject of this photograph, taken in Oswestry sometime around 1981 or 1982. The bus, a Bristol LH6L with ECW bodywork, had started life with Midland General. Forming the backdrop is the Railway Inn, still trading at the time of writing, though Border Ales, brewed in Wrexham, have long since vanished. By 1982, Hampson's, along with Vaggs Coaches (see page 49) became part of the TE Jones Group, which ceased trading that year.

Based in the Telford area, Elcock Reisen has been trading since 1928. Reisen is the German (and Dutch) word for 'Travel'. Tours, holidays and private hire jobs have long been the company's raison d'être, but some stage carriage work was being carried out in March 2001, when W166 PNT was photographed. Bought new in 2000, this Plaxton-bodied Dennis Dart is seen having a rest in Telford bus station prior to returning to Shrewsbury on route X96.

Another operator to begin trading in 1928 was Arthur Boulton, from the Shropshire village of Cardington. For many years, a sizeable amount of stage carriage work was undertaken using coaches from within the fleet. This example, fitted with 'grant-aid' folding doors, EAW 360L, was photographed in central Shrewsbury circa 1974. It is Bedford YRQ with a Plaxton forty-five-seat body.

Much less suitable for bus service operations was Arthur Boulton's SUB 668G, a 1969-built Bedford VAL70 bodied by Plaxton. It had been new to Woburn Garage of London WC1 and was photographed in Shrewsbury in 1987.

Looking rather anonymous in Shrewsbury in mid-1985 is Boulton's PUJ 291X. A Ford R1114/ Duple fifty-three-seat coach, complete with folding doors, it had been new to the company in 1982.

The products of Optare later became firm favourites in the Boulton's fleet. One of the earliest of these was D728 PUJ, a Volkswagen LT55/Optare City Pacer twenty-five-seat minibus. It was photographed at its Shrewsbury terminus in the summer of 1987.

This thirty-one-seat Optare StarRider saloon, based on a Mercedes 811D chassis, G838 LWR, is seen awaiting a run to Wem in Shrewsbury in spring 1995, when it was around five years old.

One of Optare's most popular products, the Solo midibus, has proved useful in the Boulton's fleet. Twenty-nine-seat example T645 HBF was new to the company in 1999. It was photographed in Shrewsbury bus station in July of that year.

Another Optare vehicle bought new by Boulton's was this forty-two-seat Excel low-floor saloon, registered DS52 AXF. Here it is awaiting its next duty in Shrewsbury in March 2004. Boulton's, at the time of writing, are still very much in business, but no longer operate any significant amount of stage carriage work.

Vaggs Coaches were based at the delightfully named village of Knockin Heath, deep in rural Shropshire. An eclectic collection of vehicles was employed and a good example is seen here at Shrewsbury circa 1975. Registered BVO 21C, it is an ex-Barton Bedford SB5 with forty-one-seat Harrington coachwork.

Another second-hand vehicle, FVJ 900D, had been originally delivered to Herefordshire operator Yeomans. By the mid-1970s, it had been sold to Vaggs Coaches and was photographed in Shrewsbury. This forty-five-seat vehicle, to dual-purpose standard, was a Bedford VAM5 with bodywork by Duple Midland.

Staying at Shrewsbury in the mid-1970s, we see Vaggs' NPT 307D. This unusual Ford R192 with forty-four-seat Strachans bodywork had been new to Trimdon Motor Services in County Durham.

1961-built Bedford SB3/Duple coach WUJ 577 is the first vehicle in these pages that had been purchased new by Vaggs Coaches. By the time it was photographed it would already have been reaching its mid-teens, but was about to set out on a journey to Llanymynech in the Welsh borders.

Vaggs Coaches' Ford R192/Willowbrook DP45F saloon SMC 519F had come from an unusual source. It had been new to British Railways in 1968 for staff transport purposes. Once again, the location is Shrewsbury, in the mid-1970s.

Not all the Vaggs fleet was long in the tooth. Almost new when photographed in Shrewsbury was JAW 965N, a 1975-built Ford R1114 with Duple Dominant Express fifty-three-seat coachwork.

Here is a rather contrasting pair of vehicles in the Vaggs fleet at the depot yard in 1975. On the left is PUJ 165M, a rare Ford R1014/Marshall forty-five-seat bus. Alongside sits PUX 273, a Duple Midland-bodied Bedford C4Z1 with thirty seats. Both had been new to Vaggs, in 1974 and 1958 respectively.

While Shrewsbury was the major town served by Vaggs Coaches, the company also ran regular routes into the Shropshire town of Oswestry. It is here that we see NAW 662P passing the Railway Inn circa 1981. This forty-five-seat coach is a Ford R1014 with a Plaxton Supreme Express body. Sadly, Vaggs Coaches ceased trading in 1982.

The tiny Shropshire town of Bishop's Castle has long been known for its famous pub, the Three Tuns, where beer has been brewed since the seventeenth century. The town was also home to Valley Motor Services, who ran a regular service into Shrewsbury. Seen at its Barker Street terminus in the county town is AAW 671K, a Ford R192 with forty-five-seat Duple Viceroy Express coachwork, photographed circa 1975.

Another photograph from around 1975, this time at Valley Motor Services' depot in Bishop's Castle. XAW 915K is another Ford R192, this time with forty-eight-seat Willowbrook bodywork.

As we have already seen, Valley Motor Services bought most of its vehicles new. An exception was KSD 550F, seen on the left of this picture. This Duple Midland-bodied Ford R192 had originally been delivered to Scottish operator Paterson of Dalry. Alongside is KUX 321P, a Ford R1114/Willowbrook saloon purchased by Valley Motor Services in 1975. On the right is another Ford R114, BAW 958T, this time with Duple coachwork, which would have been just over a year old when photographed in 1980.

Folding doors, as seen on Valley Motor Services' TUX 513S, made a normal coach suitable for bus service work and also attracted a government grant! This Ford R1114/Plaxton Supreme Express coach was photographed residing in the depot yard in 1985. By then the company had passed to Worthen Motorways and the main bus route was later to pass into the hands of Minsterley Motors.

Worthen is a small village around 13 miles west of Shrewsbury and was once the home of Worthen Motorways, who had a small network of bus routes serving the border areas. Seen on the Wales side of the boundary, in Welshpool, in 1975, is YUX 681K. New to the company in 1972, it is a Ford R192 with forty-five-seat Duple Viceroy Express coachwork.

Seen at Barker Street, Shrewsbury, in 1987 is Worthen Motors (both names were used) RBD 107M. New to United Counties in 1974, this Willowbrook-bodied Bedford YRT will soon depart on a journey to Bishop's Castle.

Here we have another picture of TUX 513S (see page 54), now in the hands of Worthen Motors and seen in Shrewsbury on the former Butter's Coaches route to High Ercall. Summer 1987.

The Worthen name lived on for a few years, though the company, now named Worthen Travel, had moved to Ford, another village west of the county town. Seen departing from the bus station in Shrewsbury circa 1995 is THB 430Y, on a stage journey to Montgomery. This coach, a Plaxton-bodied DAF MB200, had been new to an operator in Cwmbran, South Wales.

Mid Wales Motorways was a sizeable operator based in Newtown, which Wikipedia states is 'the largest town in Powys'. Back in 1975, the depot yard contained plenty of interest for bus enthusiasts. On the left of this picture is EJE 92, a 1955-built Bedford SBG/Duple coach, while in the centre is MHU 49. This Bedford OB bus, with thirty-seat Duple bodywork, had been new to Bristol Tramways as long ago as 1949. In comparison, the Bedford VAS1/Duple coach on the right, registered 9162 DD, was a relative youngster, having been delivered to a Tetbury, Gloucestershire, company.

Again, we are at the yard of Mid Wales Motorways in 1975. 9162 DD, seen in the previous photograph, is on the left, while in the centre we have CEP 601D. This Duple Midland-bodied Bedford VAM5 had been bought new by the company, as had JEP 861, seen on the right. Purchased in 1959, it is a forty-one-seat Bedford SB1/Yeates combination.

Staying in 1975, this photograph was taken at Mid Wales Motorways' terminus in Welshpool. Ready for a run to Montgomery is 2804 DK, an ex-Yelloway of Rochdale Bedford SB3/Plaxton, new in 1963.

Having a rest in a yard at Welshpool in 1975 is Mid Wales Motorways' MEP 743. This Bedford SB1 with Yeates dual-purpose bodywork, containing forty-one seats, had been new to the company in 1961.

Owned by Mid Wales Motorways, LFA 31 was a twenty-nine-seat Bedford C4Z2/Duple coach that had been new to Burton Hospital in 1960. It was photographed in Welshpool on 26 March 1976. It later became a mobile home and is recorded as still being used as late as 2011. (From an original slide in author's collection, photographer unknown)

Mid Wales Motorways was purchased by Evans Coaches, from the Aberystwyth area (see page 87). The two companies were merged in 1990 and today's operations are centred on the coastal town. Branded 'Mid Wales Travel', KX07 KNW is seen in Aberystwyth on 25 July 2007. This twenty-six-seat Plaxton Primo midibus was only a couple of months old when photographed.

Cross Gates Coaches did, until 2007, run several bus services in Mid Wales, particularly in the tiny town of Llandrindod Wells, where the railway station forecourt served as a transport interchange. Seen here on 11 October 2006 is P212 RWR, a Plaxton-bodied Dennis Dart that had been new to Jaronda Travel in North Yorkshire. Behind is an Optare Alero minibus, also of Cross Gates Coaches.

New to Cross Gates Coaches, this twenty-six-seat Optare Solo, registered VX51 RBF, is also seen at Llandrindod Wells railway station on 11 October 2006.

M&D Travel was a small Shrewsbury operator partly owned, it is believed, by the Boulton family (see page 45). During its short years of stage carriage operation, it mainly used Optare products for its bus duties. New to the company in 1988, E402 YNT is seen in Shrewsbury bus station in August 1989. It is a Mercedes 811D with Optare StarRider bodywork, unusually fitted with twenty-nine coach seats.

M&D Travel also used the smaller Optare City Pacer, based on a VW LT55 chassis. The company owned at least one of these in 1987, but was also using this twenty-five-seat demonstrator, D898 NUA, seen in Shrewsbury in June of that year.

Lloyds Coaches was established as recently as 2001 and has grown to become the main operator of buses in its home town of Machynlleth. On 25 July 2007, Mercedes 709D/Alexander (Belfast) minibus P397 FEA was photographed there, passing the railway station on its way into town. This vehicle had been new to Stevenson's of Staffordshire.

Lloyds Coaches acquired the former Crosville depot in Machynlleth during 2002 and it is here, on 25 July 2007, that we see two of the company's minibuses. Closest to the camera is P222 WYN, another Mercedes 709D with Belfast-built Alexander bodywork. It had been new to Midland Red North, registered P387 FEA, in 1996. Sister vehicle P401 FEA is alongside.

Lloyds Coaches also operate into Newtown and it is here, on 5 October 2010, that we see Mercedes 814D/Plaxton minibus R812 YJC. It had been purchased from Arriva Cymru.

Larger vehicles are also included in the Lloyds Coaches fleet, such as Optare Excel saloon S168 UAL, which had been new to Trent Motor Traction. Again, the location is Newtown's small bus station, on 5 October 2010.

For many years, Williamson's ran a frequent service from Shrewsbury to the village of Pulverbatch a few miles to the south. A regular performer on the route was KWX 413, a Bedford SB built in 1951. This Duple-bodied coach had been new to Doncaster operator Kildare Coaches. It was photographed at its Barker Street terminus in 1977.

Williamson's expanded the network somewhat in the 1980s. The vehicles used on stage service work were also modernised. In mid-1985 this Leyland Leopard/Duple Dominant service bus, registered BAW 1T, was found in Shrewsbury. It had been new to one of the Shropshire Omnibus Association operators, R. A. Price.

Parked up in Shrewsbury in mid-1985 was Williamson's UUX 842S, a Bedford YMT with fifty-three-seat Plaxton Supreme Express coachwork. This had originated from fellow Shropshire operator Vaggs Coaches.

Deregulation saw Williamson's enter the 'free-for-all' and, like many other companies, introduce minibuses. In mid-1987, C167 VRE was found in Shrewsbury. In 1986 this sixteen-seat minibus had been new to Potteries Motor Traction.

Williamson's also began to operate a limited-stop service from Shrewsbury to Birmingham. About to set out on such an adventure in August 1989 was UHA 708X, a Plaxton-bodied Ford R1114 coach. It had been purchased from a Staffordshire operator.

Another Duple Dominant bus in the Williamson's fleet was HEF 362N, based on a Leyland Leopard chassis. New to Cleveland Transit, it is seen in Shrewsbury in August 1989.

On an X96 run from Shrewsbury to Birmingham, Williamson's ANA 91Y calls at Telford bus station in the summer of 1990. This vehicle, an ECW-bodied Leyland Leopard, had previously been used by Midland Red North and is illustrated on a similar working on page 8.

New to Williamson's in 1991, J327 VAW, a Carlyle-bodied Dennis Dart, is seen in Shrewsbury on a park & ride service in late 1992.

Arriving at its destination of Shrewsbury, on the long journey from Birmingham, in spring 1995, is Williamson's RGS 93R. Built for a Hampshire operator, it is a Plaxton-bodied Leyland Leopard coach.

Another Williamson's coach used on the X96 was photographed in Shrewsbury in December 1992. Bebb of Llantwit Fardre, South Wales, had originally used F44 CTX, a Leyland Tiger with Duple 320 coachwork fitted with folding doors, on similar duties.

Not every coach in the Williamson's fleet was second-hand. The company purchased M701 HBC in 1994. This fifty-seven-seat Dennis Javelin/Plaxton vehicle was photographed in Shrewsbury in the spring of 1995.

Williamson's also entered the low-floor era, by purchasing an Optare Excel saloon in 1997. A forty-seat vehicle registered P315 FAW, it was photographed passing a fine Banks's pub, the Albert, in Shrewsbury in spring 2000. Though still in Williamson's green livery, it was, by then, in the hands of Midland Red North/Arriva, who had taken over in 1998.

One of today's major independents in Shropshire is Minsterley Motors. Back in mid-1984, the company's main depot was at Stiperstones. Seen there on that occasion is YUJ 492K, a Bedford YRQ/Duple Viceroy Express forty-five-seat coach, often used on the stage carriage services.

On the same day and location as the previous photograph, Minsterley Motors' MHP 17V looks smart on a dull day. New to Shaw of Coventry, it is a Plaxton Supreme-bodied Bedford YMT.

One of the newest vehicles in the Minsterley Motors fleet in mid-1984 was WNT 746Y, a DAF MB200 with fifty-three-seat Plaxton Paramount coachwork, fitted with folding doors for bus service duties. Once again, the location is the depot yard at Stiperstones.

In the middle and later years of the 1980s, Minsterley Motors developed at preference for the Alexander 'Y' type style of bodywork. A typical example is GSX 117N, a 1975-built Bedford YRT that had been new to Lothian Regional Transport, Edinburgh's main bus operator. It is seen at Barker Street, Shrewsbury, mid-1985.

One more 'Y' type in the Minsterley Motors fleet, this time on a Leyland Leopard chassis. UMS 111J had come from another Scottish operator, Alexander (Midland), and was photographed in Shrewsbury in mid-1987.

Minsterley Motors' GNL 839N is another Leyland Leopard/Alexander 'Y' type. It had been delivered to Tyne and Wear PTE as a sixty-two-seat dual-purpose vehicle. Here, on 15 June 1989, it awaits its next duty in Shrewsbury. (Richard Huggins)

In mid-1987, Minsterley Motors' KUX 321P was photographed at its Barker Street terminus in Shrewsbury. This Ford R1114/Willowbrook saloon had come from Valley Motor Services (it is seen with that company on Page 54) and it will probably soon depart on a journey over the route to Bishop's Castle.

Not really suited to a suburban duty, Minsterley Motors' NWK 10P is seen leaving Shrewsbury bus station in spring 1995. This is another coach that had come from Shaw of Coventry and it had been new as a Bedford YLQ/Plaxton forty-five-seat coach.

Operating another Minsterley Motors' local service in Shrewsbury, in December 1992, is this Renault Master minibus, G738 VKK, caught on film as it departs from the bus station.

In the spring of 1995, Minsterley Motors' CWA 439T is seen leaving Shrewsbury bus station empty, have earlier arrived from Bishop's Castle. This Bedford YMT/Duple Dominant bus had come from Yorkshire operator Wigmore of Dinnington.

This vehicle had started life in south-east England with Tillingbourne of Cranleigh. D918 GRU, a Plaxton-bodied Bedford YMT bus, was photographed with Minsterley Motors in spring 1998, leaving Shrewsbury bus station on a short working of route 553 to Minsterley.

A similar vehicle to the previous photograph, a Bedford YMT/Plaxton bus, D913 URG, is seen in a rather garish colour scheme in Shrewsbury bus station in July 1999. This bus had been new to Tyneside operator Low Fell Coaches.

Minsterley Motors, like all of Britain's bus service providers, are now obliged to use accessible low-floor vehicles. One of these, bought new by the company in 2003, is DX03 XEC, a Wright-bodied Volvo B7RLE forty-four-seat bus. It was photographed as it turned into Shrewsbury bus station in March 2004.

Another low-floor bus in the Minsterley Motors fleet, DX57 REU, was photographed on Corve Street in Ludlow on 4 October 2010. Another Volvo B7RLE, it has Plaxton 'Centro' forty-four-seat bodywork.

A more unconventional vehicle being used by Minsterley Motors on 4 October 2010 is YN59 BKE. This thirty-three-seat Mercedes O816D/Plaxton coach is seen in Ludlow, about to depart on the infrequent 745 service to Pontesbury.

According to the company's website, 2020 marks the 100th anniversary of Tanat Valley Coaches, who operate bus services in the rural borderlands. Photographed in Oswestry in late 1992 is ABR 778S, still in the full livery (apart from the legal lettering by the entrance) of Bromyard Omnibus. This fine vehicle, a Plaxton-bodied Leyland Leopard, had been new to The Eden, a County Durham operator.

B105 KPF had started life as Berkhof-bodied Leyland Tiger coach with London Country. It was rebodied by East Lancs as a sixty-one-seat bus for further service with Midland Red North. It later passed to Tanat Valley and is seen at the company's depot, Llanrhaeadr-ym-Mochnant, on 29 April 2006.

Tanat Valley runs a sizeable network of bus routes, some of which serve Newtown. This is where N814 WGR was photographed on 5 October 2010. This Plaxton 'Verde' bodied Volvo B10B-58 had been new to Northern General.

In recent years Tanat Valley has operated a small fleet of Optare Tempo saloons bought new. An example is YJ56 ATX, seating forty-two passengers. It was photographed as it loaded up in Llanidloes on 5 October 2010.

Happy Days (Austin's) is a well-respected coach operator based in the Staffordshire village of Woodseaves. For many years the company ran a regular stage carriage service from Stafford to Donnington in Shropshire, where connections could be made with Shropshire Omnibus Association routes towards Wellington. At Donnington in 1975, JRE 721K, a Willowbrook-bodied Ford R192, is seen on arrival.

Archway Motors was a company based in the small Shropshire town of Shifnal. A small amount of bus service work was undertaken and, in 1975, the regular performer was KDB 647. This Weymann-bodied Leyland Tiger Cub had been new to North Western Road Car as No. 647 in 1956. It was photographed at its terminus, a bit of spare ground on the edge of Shifnal.

Horrock's, based at Lydbury North, once ran a few services in rural Shropshire, including routes into Shrewsbury. That is where we see PGX 235L, photographed in late 1992. This Ford R192/ Willlowbrook saloon had been new to London operator Continental Pioneer, who had used it to operate the 'Hill Service' in Richmond.

In spring 1995 Horrock's ex-Ribble Fiat/Iveco 49.10 minibus, bodied by Robin Hood, D625 BCK, enters Shrewsbury bus station to take up a service on route 54 to Bishop's Castle.

Trefaldwyn, meaning 'The Town of Baldwin', is the Welsh name for Montgomery. That small town was once the home of Trefaldwyn Motors. In mid-1985 the company had a small network of stage carriage services and a regular performer on such duties was Bedford YMT/Duple Dominant fifty-nine-seat bus KUJ 125W. Bought new in 1980, it is seen at the depot alongside two Bedford coaches.

At Trefaldwyn Motors' depot in mid-1985 is ex-Grampian (Aberdeen) dual-doored Leyland National KSO 76P. Sadly, Trefaldwyn Motors has since ceased trading.

Bryn Melyn Motor Services was a small independent based in Llangollen. After deregulation, etc., the company expanded somewhat and began operations into Shropshire. At Oswestry bus station in December 1992 we see PMT-bodied Mercedes 709D minibus E795 CCA. It had been delivered to the company in 1988 with twenty-five coach seats.

On 7 October 2010 Bryn Melyn's W235 CDN is seen just after leaving Shrewsbury bus station for Ellesmere. This Ikarus-bodied DAF SB220 had been new to one of the operators on the Scottish island of Great Cumbrae. At the time of this photograph Bryn Melyn Motor Services had sold out to GHA Coaches, but retained its separate identity until 2015.

West Midlands operator Choice Travel ventured into Shropshire in the early years of the twenty-first century. At Telford bus station in mid-2003 we see Leyland Tiger/Duple coach XUX 275Y. It had been transferred from fellow Status Group operator Border Buses from Lancashire.

Choice Travel's twenty-nine-seat Optare Solo YN53 ELV was found outside the Golden Lion pub in Bridgnorth in July 2004, ready for a run down the Severn Valley to Kidderminster. Choice Travel was later taken over by D&G Bus of Staffordshire.

Pete's Travel was another post-deregulation operator based in the West Midlands. Some of its tendered work took it into Shropshire and R659 GCA was photographed in Bridgnorth High Street in July 2004 on a working to Shrewsbury. This Dennis Dart SLF/Plaxton saloon had been new to a Knutsford, Cheshire, operator.

In 2005 the trading name of Pete's Travel became People's Express. Carrying that lettering is KU52 RYM, a thirty-seven-seat Dennis Dart SLF/Plaxton bought new in 2002. It was photographed departing Shrewsbury bus station on route 437 to Bridgnorth not long before the company was sold to the Birmingham Coach Company.

Messrs Parish of Oswestry ran a few services in and around its home town. Seen alongside the impressive, but closed, railway station circa 1975 is TUX 913J. This ex-Whittle's Duple Viceroy-bodied Bedford YRQ is about to depart on a service to Llanfyllin.

Parish's depot was situated at the village of Morda, on the outskirts of Oswestry. Here, in 1977, we see 272 STF, an ex-Lancashire United AEC Reliance with dual-purpose Plaxton bodywork. Most of the Parish business was sold in 1982, to Owen's Coaches, though some minibus operations were retained.

Charles Butter founded his bus and coach firm in 1927, based in the Shropshire village of Childs Ercall. A regular service into the county town was operated, with a great variety of vehicles, over the years. When this photograph was taken in mid-1985, fifty-three-seat Bedford YMT/Duple Dominant coach, registered YUJ 416T, was in use. It is seen at its Shrewsbury terminus. In the early years of the twenty-first century the centre of operations moved to Market Drayton.

Evans Coaches, of Penryncoch, ran a service into Aberystwyth and, in 1977, was using OEJ 585K on this duty. New to the company in 1972, this Bedford YRQ had a forty-five-seat Duple Viceroy Express body. It is seen leaving its Aberystwyth terminus.

Owen's Coaches, still in business today, are based in the Shropshire town of Oswestry, but run several bus services in and around Welshpool and Newtown. Back in the summer of 1987, however, the company also served its home town and that is where we see MUG 522L. This Plaxton-bodied Leyland Leopard coach had, unusually, been new to a municipal operator, Leeds City Transport.

Also from the Leeds area, a former West Yorkshire PTE vehicle, still wearing that organisation's full livery. Owned by Owen's, C807 KBT, an Optare-bodied Leyland Cub, was photographed on the town service in Oswestry in summer 1987.

A rare vehicle in the Owen's fleet was DX55 PKO, an Iveco 65C15 with UNVI 'logo' twenty-four-seat bodywork. It was a regular performer on the Welshpool town service and was photographed on such a duty on 29 April 2006.

Owen's also operate the town service in Newtown and, on 5 October 2010, BV57 MTK was in charge. This unusual BMC 'Hawk' 900 twenty-seven-seat bus was photographed arriving at the bus station.

A subsidiary of Owen's was Stratos Travel, based in Newtown, who operated the town service there. On such a duty at the town's small bus station in summer 2003 is W564 JVV. This twenty-nine-seat Dennis Dart SLF/Plaxton had been bought new in 2000. (Jim Sambrooks)

Based in Llanidloes, Celtic Travel operates a number of bus services in Wales, but also runs the X75 service into Shrewsbury. On such a working, passing the excellent Salopian Bar, Smithfield Road, in Shrewsbury, is BG61 SXW. This fine Wright-bodied Volvo B7RLE was photographed on 11 January 2020. (Barrie Gilbert)

Celtic Travel also operates several schools contracts and M239 XWS is dedicated to such duties. An ex-Ministry of Defence Dennis Javelin/Wadham Stringer bus, it was capable of seating seventy students. Originally registered CX 63 AA, it was photographed in Caersws on 5 October 2010.

Brown's Coaches of Builth Wells once ran several stage carriage services throughout rural Mid Wales. Just arrived in Newtown bus station on 5 October 2010 was R162 GNW. This Plaxton-bodied DAF SB3000 had been new to Armchair Passenger Transport of London.

Back in the summer of 1989, a firm trading as B-Line was operating the short-lived 'Rail Link' service on behalf of Shropshire County Council. B242 AFV, a sixteen-seat Mercedes 508D minibus used on this service, was photographed departing from Shrewsbury bus station.

Jones of Llandyllin was operating a stage carriage service into Oswestry when this photograph was taken in the summer of 1987. The vehicle is an ex-Maidstone Borough Council Bedford YLQ/Duple Dominant bus registered WKM 70S.

R&B Travel runs several routes around Ludlow, including the town service. Optare Solo buses are employed and V11 RBT, a twenty-seven-seat example, was photographed in Ludlow in March 2003.

The village of Threapwood is situated in Cheshire, close to the Welsh border. It was home to Huxley Travel, who operated into the Shropshire towns of Wem and Whitchurch. At the latter's small bus station in mid-1987 is PUF 257M. New to Southdown, it is a Duple Dominant coach-bodied Ford R1114.

King Offa Travel was a short-lived independent that operated into Shrewsbury from Mid Wales. Seen at its Shropshire destination in spring 1995 is DDM 22X, an ex-Crosville Leyland Leopard/ Willowbrook coach.

Foxall's Coaches was once a Bridgnorth-based operator with a garage and coach station on Underhill Street. The company undertook a small amount of stage carriage work, including services to RAF Stanmore and Norton. It is the latter that is the destination for ANT 283L, a Willowbrook-bodied Ford R192, fitted with coach seats, seen in Bridgnorth town centre in 1974. The bus stop was very handy for the pub! Shortly afterwards the Foxall's business was sold to the Whittle Group.

Shropshire County Council once ran a few buses, mainly catering for schools duties. On such a working in Ludlow on 4 October 2010 is sixteen-seat Volkswagen Crafter minibus SN58 BZD. This vehicle was later sold to Sheffield Community Transport.

During the late 1980s a special service was operated around the industrial archaeology sites and a park & ride facility in the Ironbridge area using heritage vehicles. Richard Huggins was in attendance on 26 July 1987 and photographed Bedford OB/Duple coach BJV 590 at Coalport. Owned by Kestrel Coaches of Worcester, it had been new in 1950 to a Grimsby business.

Also on such duties, on the same day, was UJT 384. Owned at the time by M Stanton of Church Stretton, this Bedford SBG/Duple coach had been new in 1956 to Greenslades of Devon, registered SFJ 904. After a spell in Jersey it came back to the mainland as GRE 63T. Richard Huggins photographed it in Ironbridge town centre.

One non-PSV operation in Shropshire just *has* to have a page dedicated to it. JP Wood & Sons provided staff transport for its Chuckie Chickens operation at Craven Arms. Used on such duties and photographed at Craven Arms in 1975 was MXX 364. This ECW-bodied Guy Special had started life with London Transport as GS64 in 1953.

JP Wood & Sons' 349 NKT was found in Bishop's Castle on a sunny day in mid-1978. This Weymann-bodied AEC Reliance had been new to Maidstone & District as No. S349 in 1961. The Chuckie Chickens business closed in the early 1990s.